I0162529

The Prophetic Unlocking

Intercessors Devotional Series 101

"Be Blessed" Prophetic Prayer Decrees and Declarations

Declaring War For Your Destiny Through Prophetic Prayer Decrees and Declarations

Copyright © November 13, 2015

By Apostle Dr. Nadine Manning

ISBN 978-0-989-8369-3-7

Printed in the USA by

Prophetic in Warfare Deliverance & Worship Tabernacle in association with Kingdom Graphics Designo Inc.

P.O. Box 343, Millville, New Jersey 08332
apostlenadineglobal@gmail.com

The Prophetic Unlocking

Intercessors Devotional ~ Series 101

"Be Blessed" Prophetic Prayer Decrees and Declarations

Declaring War For Your Destiny Through Prophetic Prayer Decrees and Declarations

By: Apostle Dr. Nadine Manning

Contents

Setting The Atmosphere

The number twenty-two (22), is significant as to this series of "The Prophetic Unlocking, Intercessors Devotional." There are approximately twenty-two (22) Prophetic Prayer Decrees and Declaration compiled in this series. Twenty-Two (22) indicates Prophetic Increase, Restoration, Restitution, and Breakthroughs not just double, but **"DOUBLE-DOUBLE."**

Isaiah 61:7 declares that, **"For your shame ye shall have double; and for confusion they shall rejoice in their portion: therefore in their land they shall possess the double: everlasting joy shall be unto them."** The double portion is symbolic to the Spirit of the first born, Jesus, the Messiah. His name means *"Anointed One."* It further reveals that the *"Double Portion"* indicates a limitless flow of the anointing. When you have the Lord as your portion, you shall receive more than double for all your services and suffering.

This is the season for God's people to experience His overwhelming favor and profuse blessings overflowing in their lives. Hence, the reason for Him constantly wooing us to draw nearer to Him.

I decree and declare that for every past humiliation and suffering you shall be doubly rewarded.

Salvation

For those who have turned away from the Lord or you have never received Him as your personal Lord and Savior, now is the set time of God's Favor. He is releasing His mercy towards you to heal you and restore your land with doubly rewards, if only you be willing and obedient.

St. John 14:12 reveals Jesus said, ***"I tell you the truth, anyone who believes in me will do the same works I have done, and even greater works, because I am going to be with the Father."***

You have to believe that Jesus Christ is the son of God before you can even begin to make these decrees and declarations of faith.

-

Romans 10:8-13 says: ***"But what saith it? The word is nigh thee, even in thy mouth, and in thy***

heart: that is, the word of faith, which we preach; 9 That if thou shalt confess with thy mouth the Lord Jesus, and shalt believe in thine heart that God hath raised him from the dead, thou shalt be saved. 10 For with the heart man believeth unto righteousness; and with the mouth confession is made unto salvation. 11 For the scripture saith, Whosoever believeth on him shall not be ashamed. 12 For there is no difference between the Jew and the Greek: for the same Lord over all is rich unto all that call upon him. 13 For whosoever shall call upon the name of the Lord shall be saved.

1. You must have a personal relationship with Jesus Christ to walk into and speak faith.

2. It is by His grace that we are saved, not of ourselves. It is a gift from God to us.

3. Salvation is free to all who willing accept Jesus Christ as their Lord and Savior. St. John 3:16 tells us that,

   "For God loved the world so much that he gave his one and only Son, so that everyone who believes in him will not perish but have eternal life."

Salvation means: Deliverance of God. It is by the confession of your mouth that you experience and encounter deliverance and breakthroughs by the shed blood of Jesus Christ.

Therefore, if you do not know Jesus Christ as your personal Lord and Savior, accept Him today in your heart and be ye transformed by the power of our Lord Jesus Christ.

He takes no pleasure in those that drawback. If you are a backslider, re-dedicate your life to Him today, so that you can experience His goodness profusely, abounding and overflowing in your life again.

That being said, before you pray any of these Prophetic Decrees and Declarations, accept, or re-dedicate your life to the Lord today and watch God change things in your life for His glory.

Romans 8:28 reminds us that ***"And we know that God causes everything to work together for the good of those who love God and are called according to his purpose for them."***

SALVATION PRAYER

Dear God in heaven, I come to you in the name of Jesus. I acknowledge to You that I am a sinner, and I am sorry for my sins and the life that I have lived; I need your forgiveness.

I believe that your only begotten Son Jesus Christ shed His precious blood on the cross at Calvary and died for my sins, and I am now willing to turn from my sin.

You said in Your Holy Word, Romans 10:9 that if we confess the Lord our God and believe in our hearts that God raised Jesus from the dead, we shall be saved.

Right now I confess Jesus as the Lord of my soul. With my heart, I believe that God raised Jesus from the dead. This very moment I accept Jesus Christ as my own personal Savior and according to His Word, right now I am saved.

Thank you Jesus for your unlimited grace which has saved me from my sins. I thank you Jesus that your grace never leads to license to sin, but rather it always leads to repentance.

Lord Jesus transform my life so that I may bring glory and honor to your name alone and not to myself.

Thank you Jesus for dying for me and giving me eternal life. AMEN

The Prophetic Unlocking

Introduction

Where It All Began

The Prophetic Unlocking started in the beginning in Genesis Chapter One.

"In the beginning God created the heaven and the earth. ² And the earth was without form, and void; and darkness was upon the face of the deep. And the Spirit of God moved upon the face of the waters. ³ And God said, Let there be light: and there was light" [Genesis 1:1-3].

The key word is *"created."* God shaped, formed, fashioned, generated, and made something out of nothing tangible but by His

Spirit He spoke a creative word that brought forth life.

Genesis 2 reveals that, *"the earth was without form, and void; and darkness was upon the face of the deep. And the Spirit of God moved upon the face of the waters."*

God spoke to the atmosphere and a creative explosion and manifestation took place for six days, suddenly.

The same Spirit power that existed, in the beginning is available to all believers according to St. John 1:12: -*"But as many as received him, to them gave he power to become the sons of God, even to them that believe on his name."*

The "Shift" into the wonderful blessings and breakthrough God has for instore for you, will be made manifested out of your mouth.

"The Prophetic Unlocking" **Prophetic Prayer Decrees and Declaration** creates an atmosphere for a visitation from the Holy Spirit. This was evident in the beginning when God created the heaven and the earth.

Prophetic Prayer Decrees and Declaration proclaimed in faith, helps to drive a wedge into Satan plots and destroys the demonic and diabolical assignments of the enemy.

Your prayers increases and raises a standard for supernatural encounters and visitation as you build up and grow in your relationship with God the Father through the Holy Spirit.

Our prayers and supplications made in faith drives fear upon our adversary, Satan. God delights in our prayers and the Angels of the Lord respect it and are positioned and ready to execute that which you are decreeing and declaring in faith.

The most powerful way to birth out the ultimate and greater destiny in your lives and the lives of others you are believing God for is through Prophetic Decrees and Declaration.

- I declare to you, that God will get the Glory out of your life. Your trials, tribulation or test though painful, are not in vain. God knows how to "**SHIFT**" things around and get you where you are supposed to be "**SUDDENLY**."

- I decree and declare that God has not changed His mind about blessing you with the right person.

- I decree and declare to you that God has not changed His mind about blessing you with that business, or to heal you.

- I decree and declare to you that God has not changed His mind about restoring your marriage, or your family.

- I decree and declare to you that God has not changed His mind about that bigger home or new house.

- I decree and declare to you that, what looks like death, is just a set up for the **"Suddenlies of God"** to be made manifest in your life in Jesus name, Amen.

The Prophetic Unlocking – Prophetic Prayer Decrees and Declaration allows you to put your **"Faith In Action"** by the confessions of your mouth.

In order to possess our possession we need the rain of God's presence. This is the time, this is the season, and this is the hour of breakthrough, release, signs and wonders in the midst of God's people. Prophetic Prayer Decrees and Declarations made in **"Faith"** takes back by force that which the devil stole from you.

The Prophetic Unlocking has to do with breaking through the darkness of this age, unleashing the power and presence of God to set free them that are bound, to declare the acceptable year of the Lord and so much more.

You have the power to change your atmosphere and those around you by decrees and declarations made in faith under an **"Open Heaven."** Open means: - Unfasten, to expose or to unlock.

We serve a God that have given us the "**Keys**" to the "**Prophetic Unlocking.**"

In the book of Isaiah Chapter 40, God promised restoration to the Israelites. It was during a time when they faced adverse situations.

What adverse situations are you facing right now? Understand this, the seeds of comfort must take root in the soil of adversity. When you go through a wilderness experience, it comes to perfect your faith. It is during this season of waiting you learn to adapt your faith to the challenges by my making **"Prophetic Prayer Decrees and Declarations"** until something supernatural happens.

The Prophetic Unlocking speaks to dominion authority given to us by the power of our Lord Jesus Christ to bind and loose.

This is the season, this is the hour that you must take by force your destiny and the healing of the nations. Matthew 11:12 declares that, **"And from the days of John the Baptist until now the kingdom of heaven suffers violence, and the violent take it by force."**

The Lord will give you supernatural strength in this season to bind and loose when the enemy tries to buffet you. As Matthew 18:18 declares, **"Whatsoever ye shall bind on earth shall be bound in heaven: and whatsoever** *ye shall loose on earth shall be loosed in heaven."*

Romans 10:8 also declares that, *"The word is near you, in your mouth and in your heart" that is, the word of faith which we preach."* We serve a God of times and seasons. The Holy Spirit is still using the Prophetic Grace to unlock people's destiny, as well as new times and seasons.

When trials and tribulation comes upon you it pushes you to press or move forward into the supernatural. As the scripture declares that, *"From the time of John the Baptizer until now, the kingdom of heaven has been forcefully advancing and the forceful people have been seizing it."*

When Paul and Silas was in prison bound in chains and their feet were placed in stocks, they were pushed into a position to *"Take it by force!"* Your spiritual position in Christ is your God-given authority to take by force what the devil took from you through Prophetic Decrees and Declaration.

Your tests and trials forces you to advance. It pushes you to rise up out of the *"Valley of Dry Bones."* by the decrees and declarations that flows out of your belly and through your mouth.

> *"The hand of the Lord came upon me and brought me out in the Spirit of the Lord, and set me down in the midst of the valley; and it was full of bones. 2 Then He caused me to pass by them all around, and behold, there were very many in the open valley; and indeed they were very dry. 3 And He said to me, "Son of man, can these bones live?" So I answered, "O Lord God, You know." 4 Again He said to me,*

Prophesy to these bones, and say to them, 'O dry bones, hear the word of the Lord! 5 Thus says the Lord God to these bones: "Surely I will cause breath to enter into you, and you shall live. 6 I will put sinews on you and bring flesh upon you, cover you with skin and put breath in you; and you shall live. Then you shall know that I am the Lord." 7 So I prophesied as I was commanded; and ass I prophesied, there was a noise, and suddenly a rattling; and the bones came together, bone to bone" [Ezekiel 37:1-7].

No matter how dry or dead it maybe, if you believe and stand upon the word of God, He will restore all things by the decrees and declaration that flows out of your mouth. St. John 7:38 affirms this saying, *"He that believeth on me, as the scripture hath said, out of his belly shall flow rivers of living water.*"

Your decrees and declarations triggers a "**Shift**" in the spiritual realm. The shift that takes place is deemed as, "**The Prophetic Unlocking**." The book of Ezekiel 37 gives a vivid description as a release of a "Prophetic Wind" through the Prophetic Decrees and Declarations made by Ezekiel to the **"Valley of Dry Bones."**

> *"Then said he unto me, Prophesy unto the wind, prophesy, son of man, and say to the wind, Thus saith the Lord GOD; Come from the four winds, O breath, and breathe upon these slain, that they may live. 10 So I prophesied as he commanded me, and the breath came into them, and they lived, and stood up upon their feet, an exceeding great army*" [Ezekiel 37:9-10].

You have the power to change your circumstances by the confession of your mouth. You may not escape adversity but you may find comfort as you face it, by coming into agreement with God's word and promises.

Romans 10:10 also declares that, **"For it is by believing in his heart that a man becomes right with God; and with his mouth he tells others of his faith, confirming his salvation."**

Your Prophetic Prayer Decrees and Declarations spoken in the atmosphere reveals to others the level of your **"Faith."**

As a result it allows them to come into agreement with those decrees and or declarations.

I would like to take this opportunity to admonish all the Five-Fold leaders in the Kingdom, Worshippers, Praise Dancers,

Musicians, Gate-Keepers/Intercessors, Missionaries and all lay-workers that the healing of the nation also belongs to us as people of God.

But first we must return from our backsliding hearts. The idols in our hearts must come down. If we are not confident about what we belief and finding comfort in God's word and promises for ourselves we cannot be effective *"Gatekeepers on the Walls of Prayer."*

Can't you see what is happening the enemy is slowly trying to get those who are not established, rooted and grounded in their hope and faith in God's word to compromise their belief, standard and principles of God word for inclusion of sinful practices at all levels in our churches. You must arise and be bold in your faith and make confessions of God's promises from your mouth.

of God [Romans 10:8-12].

This is what will maintain, strengthen and support you when adversities arise, even test, or temptations.

2 Timothy 2:1-2 [ESV] admonishes us saying: -

"You then, my child, be strengthened by the grace that is in Christ Jesus, 2 and what you have heard from me in the presence of many witnesses entrust to faithful men[a] who will be able to teach others also."

2 Timothy 3:1-7 [ESV] also explains: -

"But understand this, that in the last days there will come times of difficulty. 2 For people will be lovers of self, lovers of money, proud, arrogant, abusive, disobedient to their parents, ungrateful, unholy, 3 heartless,

unappeasable, slanderous, without self-control, brutal, not loving good, 4 treacherous, reckless, swollen with conceit, lovers of pleasure rather than lovers of God, 5 having the appearance of godliness, but denying its power. Avoid such people. 6 For among them are those who creep into households and capture weak women, burdened with sins and led astray by various passions, 7 always learning and never able to arrive at a knowledge of the truth."

God is not a God to lie to you. He is a Promise-Keeper. He watches over His word to perform it according to Jeremiah 1:12. That which He has spoken will not return to Him void of power. Isaiah 46:11 [ASV] also declares, *"I have spoken, I will also bring it to pass; I have purposed, I will also do it."*

Don't be disheartened by what you see happening around you. These things are just the signs of the time. Remain steadfast, immovable, always abounding in the work of the Lord. Appreciate the comfort and encouragement found in God's word, use them to establish your Prophetic Prayer Decrees and Declaration and watch God change things.

Here are two vital scriptures to remind you and stir your hearts once again.

> *"I looked for a man among them who would build up the wall and stand before Me in the place where it is broken, to stop Me from destroying the land, but I found no one"* [Ezekiel 22:30].

> *"On your walls, O Jerusalem, I have put men to keep watch. All day and all night they will never be quiet. You who help the Lord remember, do not*

rest. 7 And give Him no rest until He builds Jerusalem and makes it praise in the earth" [Isaiah 62:6].

We can only be effective at this if we come back to a heart of *"True Worship."* There needs to be a serious stirring of our hearts once again to raise the banner of Jesus Christ through Prophetic Decrees and Declaration.

We must also take our rightful place as priests in our homes and decree and declare the will of God, blessings, healing and deliverance over our children and loved ones. Only those who do the work will reap the benefits.

Listen to what Isaiah 62:8-9, [NLV] declares, *"The Lord has sworn by His right hand and by His strong arm, "I will never again give your grain to be food for those who hate you. And strangers will never again drink your new wine that you have worked hard to make. 9 But those who have worked on it will eat it and praise the Lord. And those who gather it will drink it in the open spaces inside My holy house."*

I declare to you this day the Spirit of the Lord says *"Arise Shine for the Light has come and the Glory of the Lord has risen upon you."*

- You were *"Chosen for This."*
- You were *"Made For This."*
- You are *"Anointed For This".*

The Prophetic Unlocking

Prophetic Decrees and Declarations

For Divine Release

Under the authority invested in me as an Apostle and a Prophet to the Nations:-

- *I decree and declare over your life that, "God is reversing somethings in your life according to Daniel chapter 6. I decree and declare a "Divine Reversal" of every plot and scheme of the enemy over your life. I decree and declare that God is shutting the Lion mouth right now in the name of Jesus.*

- *I decree and declare that just as the Israelites shoes nor clothing wore out during their wilderness wandering but kept them, so the "UNLIMITED SOURCE" of God has been maintaining you and will not run out.*

- *I decree and declare that as you continue to walk in obedience to God's divine will for your life, you shall experience a continuous flow of supernatural release, intervention and , blessings miracles in your life, business and ministry.*
- *I decree and declare that God is about to interrupt the flow and order of diabolical assignments, traps that has been sent to take you off course.*
- *I decree and declare that your DAYBREAK" is here and God has stepped in to interrupt and reverse something's on your behalf in the name of Jesus.*
- *I decree and declare that your enemies shall be your footstool in the name of Jesus.*
- *I decree and declare the blessings of the Lord upon you.*
- *I decree and declare that with favor, will [He] surround you as with a shield.*
- *I decree and declare "The Prophetic Unlocking" of your breakthrough, your healing, your financial success and increase.*
- *I decree and declare that this is the hour of supernatural visitation for your*

"Divine Release and Uncommon Favor through these Prophetic Prayer Decrees and Declaration in Jesus name, amen!

Chapter 1

The Watchman's Position

A Watchman speaks for the Lord. A Watchman is a Gatekeeper for his or her city and the nations assigned to him to stand in the gap for with intercessory prayer. A watchman is also a Gatekeeper for their churches and families. When a Watchman makes **Prophetic Prayer Decrees and Declaration** they speak for the Lord translating the sound of heaven into the earth. This is formed, manifested and released out of an abiding relationship with the Lord.

> *"Abide in me, and I in you. As the branch cannot bear fruit of itself, except it abide in the vine; no more can ye, except ye abide in me. ⁵ I am the*

vine, ye are the branches: He that abideth in me, and I in him, the same bringeth forth much fruit: for without me ye can do nothing. ⁶ If a man abide not in me, he is cast forth as a branch, and is withered; and men gather them, and cast them into the fire, and they are burned. ⁷ If ye abide in me, and my words abide in you, ye shall ask what ye will, and it shall be done unto you. ⁸ Herein is my Father glorified, that ye bear much fruit; so shall ye be my disciples."

Your decrees and declaration go forth and produce, bearing fruits as well as reproduce. Signs and wonders will follow prophetic utterances through your decrees and declaration, releasing the manifestations of miracles because of your abiding relationship with the Lord. An abiding relationship indicates that you are constantly being pruned to grow, to continually be a carrier of the Glory of God.

The Watchman releases goodness, proclaims salvation and says to Zion, "*Your God Reigns*!" The Apostolic and Prophetic Anointing is for Kingdom Purpose and Assignment to release God's people.

Re-Wired To The Promise

We need to be "Re-Wired to the Promises of God. For us to get "Re-Wired" to the Promise we must get back to the true and solid foundation of the church.

The Biblical foundation of the church is the Apostles and Prophets, Jesus Christ the chief cornerstone.

> *"Now, therefore, you are no longer strangers and foreigners, but fellow citizens with the saints and members of the household of God, [20] having been built on the foundation of the apostles*

and prophets, Jesus Christ Himself being the chief cornerstone" [Ephesians 2:19-20].

The church has moved away from the foundation of the voice of the Apostles and Prophets. We are in an era or time in the church where God wants to rebuild and restore what has been torn down as the basic principles of our faith.

2 Chronicles 20:20b says *"Believe in the Lord your God, and you shall be established; believe His prophets, and you shall prosper."*

The Army of Jehoshaphat sought the Lord in prayer and fasting for a few days as one strong army. Their leader King Jehoshaphat who carried an Apostolic Anointing made certain Prophetic Prayers Decrees and Declarations fueled by faith unto the Lord.

As a result of those decrees and declarations made under an open heaven by

King Jehoshaphat their leader and the power of agreement in the midst of the people, God released Divine Instructions and Divine Strategies through the prophet [Read 2 Chronicles 20:5-17]. They believed the Prophet and they moved out in *"Faith."* Their response to the **"Prophetic Voice"** not only raised up a great army, but they had constant victories as they continued to yield to the voice of the prophets.

Furthermore, they walked in supernatural prosperity and success. God fought for their battles and defeated their enemies and they collected the spoils and reaped their enemies' blessings.

The blessings of the Lord were overflowing its banks as a result of this, it took them three (3) days to collect the spoils.

"When Jehoshaphat and his people came to take away their spoil, they found among them an abundance of

valuables on the dead bodies, and precious jewelry, which they stripped off for themselves, more than they could carry away; and they were three days gathering the spoil because there was so much. 26 And on the fourth day they assembled in the Valley of Berachah, for there they blessed the Lord" [2 Chronicles 20:25-26].

God is raising up a **"Prophetic Company"** and a **"Prophetic Army"** that shall bring restoration to the church of the living God.j

It is a *"Prophetic Company and a Prophetic Army"* who will be sensitive to the Prophetic Wind and Supernatural Stirring of the Lord under an *"Open Heaven."*

There is a **"Prophetic Company"** and **"Prophetic Army"** rising up to bring change.

We will experience the visitations of the Lord with the rain of His presence that will release lasting and effective change in the nations of this world. He is raising up a remnant who will hearken to the voice of the Lord. Now is the acceptable year of the Lord. The time to get *"Re-Wired"* to the promise is NOW!

There Shall Be A Breaking Forth

I hear the Lord says, there shall be a *"BREAKING FORTH."*

"Thy watchmen shall lift up the voice; with the voice together shall they sing: for they shall see eye to eye, when the Lord shall bring again Zion" [Isaiah 52:8].

The watchman carries the revealed Glory of the Lord that *"Shall see eye to eye when the Lord shall bring back Zion."* You are *"Anointed For This."* I prophecy to you, *"Arise oh ye watchman of the Lord, gird up your lions with truth, God's word is truth."*

The Watchman carries the promises of God in his lions, never losing focus regardless of the pitfalls, traps, challenges or stormy trials. Jesus Christ, the chief of all watchmen, suffered because of His obedience to the will of the Father to the "*Point of death, even unto death on the cross.*"

When you make up your mind to walk in total obedience to the Lord you will experience tremendous suffering for the call and purpose that God has set for your life. Be encouraged and strengthened that:

> *"If the world hate you, ye know that it hated me before it hated you. ¹⁹ If ye were of the world, the world would love his own: but because ye are not of the world, but I have chosen you out of the world, therefore the world hateth you. ²⁰ Remember the word that I said unto you, The servant is not greater than his*

lord. If they have persecuted me, they will also persecute you; if they have kept my saying, they will keep yours also. 21 But all these things will they do unto you for my name's sake, because they know not him that sent me"

[St. John 15:18-21].

According to Philippians 3:10, suffering just propels you into a greater position of power that you have never known before.

What Is Your Mind-Set?

- *Old things are passed away and behold all things are made new. .*
- *I am no longer a prisoner to what I did or the way I use to live.*
- *I am no longer a prisoner of my past.*
- *I am no longer a prisoner to what they did to me.*
- *I am no longer a prisoner.*

- *I am no longer a prisoner to what happened to me.*

I decree and declare that, through the above declaration, a divine reversal has been set in motion to destroy the suicidal thoughts you once had, the torments at nights of the rape or molestation will now cease, your desire to quit the ministry or disobey God's unique anointing and call on your life is destroyed, your fears, failures and low-self-esteem will no longer be a mirage in your mind or memory bank.

For the word of the Lord says, **"No weapon that is formed against thee shall prosper; and every tongue that shall rise against thee in judgment thou shalt condemn. This is the heritage of the servants of the Lord, and their righteousness is of me, saith the Lord."** [Isaiah 54:17].

Some of the things were supposed to break you! But how many know that God has **"TURNED IT!"** around to be your **"DAY-BREAK!"**

- *They thought you were going to lose your mind after your husband died!*
- *They thought you would have closed the ministry after he died.*
- *They thought you would have aborted your purpose and ministry after the death of your son or after that bitter separation or divorce, "BUT GOD!"*

  They thought you would never marry or marry again because of previous wickedness and witchcraft that hindered previous relationships or because of hurts or disappointments from past relationships.
- *They thought you were about to lose your mind during your husband or wife illness.*

- *They thought you would have lost your mind after the foreclosure, or job loss, and that you would be naked and homeless.*
- *They thought you would have closed the ministry by now after all the demonic attacks they unleashed against you to frustrate your purpose and to set you back.*

But every set back is for a comeback.

There shall be a ***"Breaking Forth"*** in your life and ministry and you shall reap the fruits of your labor done through Prophetic Prayer Decrees and Declarations made in faith.

- ***I decree and declare that your come back will be greater than your set back.***
- ***I decree and declare that your place of pain shall become your place of praise.***
- ***I decree and declare that you are about to break forth into new territories.***

- *I decree and declare that you are about to encounter the floods of God's uncommon favor and provision.*
- *I decree and declare to you that an increase in wealth, and the creative power and wisdom to advance in the kingdom and entrepreneurship is released to you now.*
- *I decree and declare, increase in our finances.*
- *I decree and declare new growth and expansion in ministry in Jesus name, Amen!*

Understand that what your haters didn't see was your "**Witness Pile**" of "**Prophetic Unlocking**" [Decrees and Declarations] that caused a swelling in the spiritual realm.

It looked like death, but it was a *"SET UP FOR THE SUDDENLIES OF GOD!"* Your decrees and declaration is being activated even now! God has interrupted your zone and He is carrying you on eagle's wings into the *"KIROS"* of an *"OPEN HEAVEN"*. The *"KIROS"* is where God is.

Your circumstances or dilemma has just pushed you into and beyond the veil for the *"Suddenlies of God"* to break forth in every area of your life.

Some of the things were supposed to break you and take you out. It was supposed to kill you, but God. I said, but God... *"If it had not been for the Lord on your side, where would I be?"* Glory to God. If God be for you, who can be against you. God is about to give you a *"Day Break."*

There shall be a *"Breaking Forth"* of God's goodness and greatness in your life like never before seen or experienced. I hear the Lord say *"Get Ready, for you are being repositioned to be blessed, you are being repositioned for success"*

Say out loud, *"I Am Anointed For This."* He is using every painful circumstance and experience to give you a breakthrough that will interrupt for good every cyclical pattern and plots of the enemy over your life.

As the word *"Day Break"* defines, God is forcing and making away through, by puncturing and penetrating everything that stood in the way of your destiny. Your next *"SHIFT"* is coming out of your mouth, your next promotion is coming out of your mouth, and your next open doors that no man can shut is coming out of your mouth.

Your mouth is the opening in your head for eating and speaking.

> *"But what does it say? "The word is near you, in your mouth and in your heart" (that is, the word of faith which we preach): 9 that if you confess with your mouth the Lord Jesus and believe in your heart that God has raised Him from the dead, you will be saved. 10 For with the heart one believes unto righteousness, and with the mouth confession is made unto salvation. 11 For the Scripture says, "Whoever believes on Him will not be put to shame"* [Romans 10:8-11].

Decree a thing and it shall be established. I need you to stop right here, stand on your feet and give a praise break. I did it several times when the command comes, even driving on the high way, I pulled over and parked the car and give a praise break. Come on now, do it, one minute praise break.

Something great is about to **"BREAK FORTH"** in your life. It's a **"Day Breaker Anointing"** moment in this atmosphere through the passages of this book into your life in the name of Jesus. Shout Glory, Hallelujah!

I touch and agree with you with the Apostolic anointing on my life in Jesus name. Now, open your mouth and begin to release your faith and take by force twenty-one (21) things that you want God to do in your life or call forth that which God has promises you that is overdue or past-due!

Tell the person next to you, call you neighbor, high five that one next to you or in your house and tell them, **"I am getting ready to give birth and it is coming forth with a triple fold dimensional manifestation and multiplication...."** Hallelujah, Shout Glory, **"It's About to Break!"**

Approved By God

The Prophetic Unlocking, break forth or manifest God's divine will in your life. Because it is supernaturally activated through your decrees and declaration, it will not look like the average man's; purpose, or blessings.

Remember Hannah? She was tenacious. Hannah waited patiently for her **"Shift"** She persevered in prayer and supplication for a long-time. But when she break forth it was **"The Suddenlies of God."** What she birth out and manifested was a man of power and purpose that had a Global Impact.

God is not a God to lie, neither the son of man to repent. That which he has promised you it shall be fulfilled. It shall come to pass.

Isaiah 46:11b affirms this: -*"I have purposed it, I will also do it."*

- No man cannot hinder you! *"Believe in the Lord your God, and you shall be established; believe His prophets, and you shall prosper."* [2 Chronicles 20:20b].

- Don't mind the chatter, some are calling all around the city and county to defame your name so people will think differently. Their behavior speaks to what they are made of.

  Ephesians 6:12 says, *"For we wrestle not against flesh and blood, but against principalities, against powers, against the rulers of the darkness of this world, against spiritual wickedness in high places. 13 Wherefore take unto you the whole armour of God that ye may be able to* *withstand in the evil day, and having done all, to stand."*

Are you more concerned about man's acceptance or approval or are you yielded and obedient to the will of God for your life with a complete **"YES."** When God speaks and directs our path it is a **"Walk of Faith!"** Let him choose your friends, your husband or wife in this season. Not what man say, but what God has approved for your life and destiny in Christ. God gives us what He thinks is best for us.

What is best for us is sometimes not what we want! But it is what God say we need and is good for us. Answer the call God place on your life, it's unique, it's distinct, it is for a set people, place and time! Don't judge your call by man's opinion. Don't allow your environment to dictate your purpose! Be like Noah, and **"Dare To Be Bold"** even in the midst of ridicule, mockery and criticism. Obey God and accept His divine plan for your life! It may not be a call like what is so familiar in the kingdom! It is unique God says! Say **'YES'** to the Lord, and He will instruct you and teach you and guide you into your promise!

Where the Lord leads you to connect and fellowship in this season is for you to complete or finish your course for the purpose and assignment He as for your life!

It may not feel like the traditional church or ministry but position yourself to serve that leader and watch God. Is it likely that, you're in position for the Lord to say to you ***"You have found favor in my eyes?"***

He expects us as His children to stand for what is right, even when everyone else may insist you are wrong. My advice to you is, obey God and confidently declare that:-***"I AM ANONTED FOR THIS"!***

Prophetic Decrees and Declarations
For Intercessors To Arise

I decree and declare the "The Stirring of God" in the hearts of everyone that will touch, read and listen to these Prophetic Prayer Decrees and Declarations.

I decree and declare that your passion and pursuit after God and His manifest promises in your life will indeed fuel your spirit to a greater level and place of intercession. I decree and declare that globally intercessors will be mighty and strong "Gatekeepers" on the "Walls of Prayer" for their family and the healing of the nations.

I decree and declare that God is calling you back to your rightful place of spiritual authority to decree a thing and it shall be established.

I decree and declare the "Stirring of God" within and upon you as you make these "Prophetic Prayer Decrees and Declarations" that there will be a supernatural release and manifestation with sign and wonders to follow.

I decree and declare according to Isaiah 8:18 that, "Here am I [you] and the children whom the Lord has given me [you]! We are for signs and wonders in Israel From the Lord of hosts, Who dwells in Mount Zion."

I decree the "Stirring of God" upon every child, mother, wife, husband, Five-Fold Ministers, Ministers at all levels, Minstrel, Intercessors and the remnant who are hungry and thirsty for more of God.

I decree and declare a "Divine Shift" in your lives according to Haggai 1:14: -
"And the LORD stirred up the spirit of Zerubbabel the son of Shealtiel, governor of Judah, and the spirit of Joshua the son of Josedech, the high priest, and the spirit of all the remnant of the people; and they came and did work in the house of the LORD of hosts, their God."

Remember, **"NOW IS YOUR SEASON, NOW IS YOUR TIME ~ TO ASK THE LORD FOR RAIN."** Get ready for the *"RAIN of His Presence"* through this Series 101 of *"The Prophetic Unlocking - Intercessors Devotional "Be Blessed" Prophetic Unlocking ~ Prayer Decrees and Prophetic Declarations."* I pray that as you read this book that you will be fueled and re-ignited.

I pray that as you open your mouth to make Prophetic Prayer Decrees and Declarations that the fire of the Holy Spirit will rain upon you and:

- *"Suddenly" yokes will be destroyed.*
- *"Suddenly" Super-sized Blessings and Breakthroughs will manifest in the name of Jesus.*

For you I am praying in Jesus name.

Prophetic Prayer and Declaration #1
Let The Word Work

"But one who looks intently at the perfect law, the law of liberty, and abides by it, not having become a forgetful hearer but an effectual doer, this man will be blessed in what he does" [James 1:25].

I declare this day that I am blessed in the city and blessed in the fields. I decree and declare I will experience God's blessings and favor upon my family, in my life and on the works of my hands.

I decree and declare that the word of God works in every area of my life. As Hebrews 4:12 declares: -

"For the word of God is quick and powerful, and sharper than any two edged sword, piercing even to the dividing asunder of soul and spirit,

and of the joints and marrow, and is a discerner of the thoughts and intents of the heart."

I decree and declare that God has not forgotten me. I decree and declare that my trials and tribulation is to prove His character inside of me. The God who created something out of nothing through the power of His word worketh through me.

I decree and declare that it is an effectual work. I decree and declare that in Him I move, live and have my being and through His mighty power I live victoriously by the word of God.

I decree and declare that I am not satisfied and content with just enough when God is calling me into a place of true spiritual abundance.

I decree and declare that, I refuse to allow man's opinion, agenda or worldviews to hinder or block my mind from seeing the full view of my destiny.

I decree and declare that I will not allow someone else lack of care or passion for the things of God deter me or hinder me from experiencing the **"GLORY."**

I decree and declare that my mind is renewed in the word of God to obey and walk by faith into the fullness of my destiny.

I decree and declare that my inheritance has been predestinated and the Lord, *"Worketh all things according to the counsel of His will"* [Ephesians 1:11b].

I decree and declare that I believe God's word regardless of how I feel about my situation because *"Faith"* comes by hearing, hearing by the word of God.

I decree and declare in whatever I do and set out to accomplish today and beyond it shall prosper in Jesus name, amen!

I decree and declare that because I love you and set my mind, heart and soul to love you and obey you with long life will you satisfy me and show me your salvation.

I decree and declare that I will live a long and full life, fulfilling my purpose and destiny in the name of Jesus. I thank you Lord that my latter will be greater than my past. I decree and declare like Job, that my latter, second half is going to be greater than my beginning.

I decree and declare that I am **"Coming Out Perfect"** into a greater place in God, and I shall experience double for my trouble.

I thank you Lord for my double portion and I command it to MANIFEST NOW, in the name of Jesus.

I decree and declare that men shall give into my bosom double blessings, good measure, presses down, shaken together and running over shall men give into my bosom.

I decree and declare that I will obey God rather than man. I decree and declare that because I am blessed I will not walk into the counsel of the ungodly, nor stand in the way of sinners, nor sit in the seat of the scornful.

I decree and declare that my delight is in the law of the Lord, and on His law do I meditate day and night.

I decree and declare that my obedience to the Lord is paying off in this season and I will be like the tree planted by the rivers of water. I decree and declare that this is a season of fruitfulness in my life, my children's lives and destiny helpers' lives.

I decree and declare that I will not suffer, I will not beg for bread in the name of Jesus.

I decree and declare that whatever I do in this season shall prosper in the name of Jesus.

I thank you Lord and I give you all the praises *that "I Am Anointed For This"* and greater is coming out of every circumstances in my life in the name of Jesus.

I decree and declare in whatever I do and set out to accomplish today and beyond it shall prosper in Jesus name, amen!

Prophetic Prayer and Declaration #2

Blessed and Highly Favored

"How blessed and graciously favored is he whose help is the God of Jacob (Israel), Whose hope is in the Lord his God" [Psalm 146:5].

I decree and declare that I am blessed and highly favored by the God of Jacob [Israel] who is my help and my hope is in the Lord his God.

I decree and declare that I am blessed with all spiritual blessings in heavenly places in Christ established before the foundation of the world. I decree and declare that everything God has for me shall manifest according to His divine plan and timing because it has been predestined for me to inherit all spiritual blessings in heaven places.

I decree and declare that God has decided long before I was formed in my mother's womb my divine and eternal destiny.

I thank you Lord that *"For as many as received Him to them gave ye power to become the sons of God, even to them that believe on his name."*

Therefore, I decree and declare that I have been given the power, authority and ability to receive God's blessings and unprecedented favor in every area of my life.

I decree and declare that, what God did for Israel He is doing right now in my life.

I decree and declare that, I have and shall continue to possess the gates of my enemies, and I shall succeed.

I decree and declare that everything that I touch shall be blessed and all shall be blessed in the name of Jesus.

I decree and declare that no weapon formed against me shall prosper. I decree and declare that the Lord has destroyed my enemies before me and even if they try to pray or speak a curse over me God will not permit it in the name of Jesus!

I decree and declare according to Joshua 24:9-11 that, *"God gave them all into [my] power"* in the name of Jesus.

I decree and declare that I am blessed and

highly favored by God and that which He has promised it shall come to pass.

I decree and declare that what God has for me is for me and my resilience and determination is undaunted in this season.

I decree and declare that the Lord is about to give me lands, blessings and financial outpouring I did not even work for according to Joshua 24:12-14.

> *"I sent hornets ahead of you to run off the two kings of the Amorites; it was not done by your bow or sword. 13 I delivered to you fields you had not worked and towns you had not built...You eat the fruit of olive trees and of grape vineyards you did not even have to plant."*

I decree and declare that there is nothing I shall put my hands to that shall be impossible in the name of Jesus.

I decree and declare, this day that the boundaries of limitations are broken, in the name of Jesus and I am released into a limitless and boundless flow of God's blessings and His overwhelming favor in Jesus name, Amen.

Prophetic Prayer and Declaration #3

God Fights For Me

Joshua 23:3 declares, ***"And you have seen all that the Lord your God has done to all these nations for your sake; for the Lord your God is He who has been fighting for you."***

I decree and declare that because it is the Lord that is fighting for me, I will enter into every blessing that was already predestinated for my life and destiny!

I decree and declare that because God fights for me I am reassured to trust Him at His word.

I decree and declare that because He fights for me I am protected from danger and anyone or anything who will attempt to high-jack my destiny in the name of Jesus!

I decree and declare that every plan of the enemy to high-jack or kidnap [capture] my destiny is destroyed in the name of Jesus. Satan is defeated and God is exalted in Jesus name!

I take back every ground I have given to the enemy because of fear and discouragement!

I boldly declare that the Lord my God fights for me and has lifted up a standard against every spirit of failure, discouragement and defeat.

I decree and declare that I am more than a conqueror through Jesus Christ our Lord who love me and gave Himself for me, Amen!

Prophetic Prayer and Declaration #4
Failure Is Not An Option

In Genesis 28:15 God says, *"I will not leave you until I have finished giving you everything I have promised you."*

 I decree and declare that, just as God sent an angel to make provision for Elijah my steps are being ordered by God, and I shall experience God's hand of favor and *"Blessings even in the Storm."*

 I decree and declare that "*Failure Is Not An Option*" in my life in the name of Jesus! I thank the Lord and believe and receive my special strengthening in this season of my life in the name of Jesus.

 I speak over myself and encourage myself in the Lord that, "*Failure Is Not An Option*" for me as a believer in Christ!

 I release this word in every area of my life where the enemy have tried to counteract me that "*FAILURE IS NOT AN OPTION*."

I decree and declare that the Angels of the Lord encampeth round about those who fear him to deliver them.

I decree and declare that God promises in His word that He will never leave me nor forsake me. I decree and declare the uncommon protection of the Lord surrounds me, my family, destiny helpers, every business project, ideas, and kingdom assignment in the name of Jesus.

I decree and declare that the Lord of host is hastening to perform that which He has promised me and has released His angels on assignment to every area of my life and He will not fail me nor leave me until all that He has spoken to me is accomplished in the name of Jesus.

I decree and declare that today my **"DESTINY"** is coming into its fullness. I decree and declare that today, my breakthrough is coming into **FRUITION** in Jesus Mighty name, Amen!

Prophetic Word

- I hear these words softly spoken yet powerful in the Spirit today that "*I Will Not Fail Thee.*"
- If God says He will not *"Fail thee,"* it means that he will complete, bring to pass and finish that which He has spoken to you.
- The Spirit of the Lord also says to tell you even in areas where there is **LACK**, provision is already being made for you!

Prophetic Prayer and Declaration #5
It Shall Be Done

"In this manner, therefore, pray Our Father in heaven, Hallowed be Your name. 10 Your kingdom come. Your will be done on earth as it is in heaven" [Matthew 6:9-10].

I praise you, because you created us to give you all the praises. I send up high praises to give you all the Glory; *"Thy kingdom come, thy will be done on earth, as it is in heaven,"* and forgive me of my trespasses as I forgive those that trespass against me.

I decree and declare that with my praise you are orchestrating a divine intervention for me and drawing me closer to you, bringing me into deeper realm of humility.

Lord I thank you that I am in need your salvation. I thank you, that as I forgive men of their trespasses, and endeavor to walk in forgiveness, you will deliver me and give me my daily bread.

I decree and declare that you Oh Lord my God, will open to me your good treasures, the heaven to give the rain to my land in its season, and bless all the work of my hands.

I decree and declare that this is my season, and this is my time. I decree and declare that it is time of harvesting and a time of planting for a constant season of release and breakthroughs in my life in the name of Jesus.

I decree and declare that all the works of my hand are blessed in the name of Jesus and you shall open to me your good treasures, the heavens to give the rain to my land in Jesus name, Amen!

Prophetic Prayer and Declaration #6
Goodness and Grace

Psalm 103:2-3 says, *"Let all that I am praise the LORD; may I never forget the good things he does for me. 3 He forgives all my sins and heals all my diseases."*

Lord I give you all the praise, as the Psalmist David extoled you, *"Bless the Lord Oh My Soul and forget not what he has done"* for me! I praise you Lord for all the benefits that flows from your mercy and grace through the shed blood of Jesus Christ!

Thank you that I am strong in your grace, always improving, and continuing to be health spiritually and physically.

Thank you for the anointing like a strong wind and force that makes me strong in your grace in Jesus name.

Thank you that I am strong in your grace that makes me fortified so as to protect me against attacks in Jesus name.

Psalm 116:12 declares, *"What shall I return to the LORD for all his goodness to me?"* This morning I reflect on all your goodness to me and my family and still I just want to praise you and give you all the Glory.

I just want to say, *"Bless the Lord, Oh My Soul"* I will worship your Holy Name! I just want to sing the highest praises - Hallelujah and thank you Lord for what you have done for us! In Jesus name Amen!

Prophetic Prayer and Declaration #7
Divine Intervention Has Come

"Walk out of the gates. Get going! Get the road ready for the people. Build the highway. Get at it! Clear the debris, hoist high a flag, a signal to all peoples! Yes! God has broadcast to all the world: "Tell daughter Zion, 'Look! Your Savior comes, Ready to do what he said he'd do, prepared to complete what he promised." Zion will be called new names: Holy People, God-Redeemed, Sought-Out, City-Not-Forsaken" [Isaiah 62:10-12].

I decree and declare that I am called by God with a new name: - *"Sought-out, City - Not - Forsaken, a Holy People, and the redeemed of the Lord."*
I thank you Lord that I am in position for my divine intervention. I decree and declare that

my Savior has come, divine intervention has come.

Lord I thank you that Isaiah 62:10-12 declares, you are ready to do what you said you would do! I decree and Lord You are prepared to complete what you have promised in my life in Jesus name, Amen!

Prophetic Prayer and Declaration #8
Walking In Divine Instructions

"You are my hiding place; You shall preserve me from trouble; You shall surround me with songs of deliverance. Selah 8 I will instruct you and teach you in the way you should go; I will guide you with My eye" [Psalm 32:7-8].

Lord you said according to Psalm 32:7 that, **"You are my hiding place"** and that you preserve me in from trouble, so thank you for keeping me safe from trouble and harm, thank you for your protection.

Thank you that your peace and anointing of preservation has kept me undisturbed from the plans of the enemy.

Thank you for giving me songs of deliverance. Thank you for divine instructions and guidance according to Psalm 32:8. Teach me and instruct me as your servant, and guide me with your eyes daily and lead me in a plain path. O Lord.

I chose to obey your every instruction and Spiritual direction. Thank you for clarity of vision so I will be more sensitive to your leading in Jesus name, Amen!

Prophetic Prayer and Declaration #9
Grace To Prosper

Psalm 1:3 says, *"He shall be like a tree planted by the rivers of water and whatsoever he doeth shall prosper."*

Thank you Lord God that whatsoever I do shall prosper. I decree and declare prosperity in every area of my life, family life, ministry projects and business projects in the name of Jesus.

I thank you Lord for the granted health, wealth and happiness I have in you.

Thank you that you did not give me a spirit of fear but a Spirit of power and of love and of a sound mind.

I trust in you Lord, and in your grace that keeps me and enable me to accomplish the things that you have ordained for me to do and walk into.

I decree and declare that I am bold strong

and unstoppable because I trust in your grace to prosper in all I do in Jesus name, Amen.

Prophetic Prayer and Declaration #10
My Inheritance Is Secured

"In Him also we have received an inheritance [a destiny—we were claimed by God as His own], having been predestined (chosen, appointed beforehand) according to the purpose of Him who works everything in agreement with the counsel and design of His will" [Ephesians 1:11].

Thank you Lord that through your finished work on the cross my inheritance is secured and established in you according to Ephesians 1:11.

I decree and declare that, my blessings and purpose has been predestined long before I was formed in my mother's womb and it is attainable through Jesus Christ.

I decree and declare that my inheritance has been predestined according to God's

*"**Divine Purpose**"* and will for my life *"**who worketh all things according to the counsel of His will.**"* Lord I thank you that my purpose has been established in Christ in the heavenly realms!

Be it resolved therefore, that God's purpose to save me, deliver me, bless me, release me, enlarge my territory, to overtake and recover all cannot be thwarted no matter what evil Satan may bring in Jesus name.

I am the head and not the tail, above and not beneath in the mighty name of Jesus, Amen!"

Prophetic Prayer and Declaration #11
God Is Able To Deliver Me

"He answered and said, Lo, I see four men loose, walking in the midst of the fire, and they have no hurt; and the form of the fourth is like the Son of God" [Daniel 3:25].

Lord I thank you that as it was revealed to King Nebuchadnezzar the enemy of the three (3) Hebrew boys that there was a fourth (4th) man in the fire with them when he cast them into the burning fiery furnace because they refused to worship his idols

I hereby decree and declare that the Holy Spirit power is loosed to intervene in my trials right now to deliver me without a burn or a scratch because there is a [Fourth Man] in the fire in the name of Jesus.

Therefore, I decree and declare that you are revealing your power and mighty hand to deliver me, and my family from every diabolical plot and attack in the name of Jesus.

I decree and declare that your uncommon protection surrounds us. Thank you for heavenly visitations right now in the midst of every great test or trial we might confront or encounter in the mighty name of Jesus name!

I decree and declare that my God is an awesome God and He reigns from heaven above with wisdom, power and love, our God is an awesome God! In Jesus name, Amen!

Prophetic Prayer and Declaration #12
The Hope Of My Calling

Ephesians 1:16 declares that, "*I have not stopped thanking God for you. I pray for you constantly, 17 asking God, the glorious Father of our Lord Jesus Christ, to give you spiritual wisdom[a] and insight so that you might grow in your knowledge of God. 18 I pray that your hearts will be flooded with light so that you can understand the confident hope he has given to those he called—his holy people who are his rich and glorious inheritance. 19 I also pray that you will understand the incredible greatness of God's power for us who believe him.*"

Verse 18 - King James Version declares, "*The eyes of your understanding being enlightened; that you may know what is the hope of His calling, what are the riches of the glory of His inheritance in the saints."*

Thank you Lord for the Spirit of wisdom and revelation in the knowledge of you. I thank you Lord for enlightening the eyes of my understanding that I may know what is hope of my calling and the riches of the Glory of your inheritance for my life, family and ministry in Jesus name.

I thank you that you are now revealing to me the exceeding greatness of your power toward me because I believe upon your word and promises to me according to the working of your mighty power in Jesus name.

Lord I thank you, that I am awaken to my destiny in Jesus name, Amen.

Prophetic Prayer and Declaration #13
God Turned It

Isaiah 51:7 declares, ***"Listen to Me, you who know righteousness, You people in whose heart is My law: Do not fear the reproach of men, Nor be afraid of their insults."***

I decree and declare that I will not fear the reproach of men nor be afraid of their insults. I decree and declare according to Isaiah 51:7 that, because I have upheld the teachings of the Lord inside of me and continuously and constantly abide in His presence:-

- ***I will pay no attention to their insults, and when mocked and men close their hearts towards me; I don't let it get me down.***
- ***[Their] insults and mockeries are moth-eaten, from brains that are termite-ridden!"***

I decree and declare that, *"my setting-things-right lasts, my salvation goes on and on and on"* because I am established in the word of God and the blood of Jesus covers me, my family and kingdom assignments!

I decree and declare **that "The LORD has acquitted me; turning back my adversaries. The LORD, is in my midst and I will not fear disaster anymore!"** I decree and declare that the cup of fury given to me to drink had been divinely reversed and returned to my adversaries to drink and shall not return to me anymore!

I decree and declare that those who bless me shall be blessed and those who curse me has cursed themselves in Jesus name - Amen!

I decree and decree that God has opened up the doors of increase and multiplication of blessings and these gates of increase, blessings and unprecedented favor shall not be shut in the name of Jesus!

The Brink Of Favor

"The Brink of Favor" Prophetic Word

Walking in obedience to a divine instruction or strategy positions you at the "***Brink of Favor.***" My encouragement to you is to: - Position yourself to do God's will and watch the manifestation and floods of His overwhelming favor and promises fulfilled in your life.

I declare to you today that you are at **"The Brink of Favor."** You are about to enter into the ***FLOOD OF GOD'S FAVOR*** without limitations. God has in store for you ***FLOODS OF BLESSINGS*** into your ***DESTINY!***

I decree and declare that you are about to experience debt cancellation, promotion, meeting that right person for your life and ministry, new open doors for business and ministry opportunities!

I hear the Lord says, somebody reading this will be moving to another state or migrating to another country to experience the "**FLOOD OF HIS FAVOR**." Your obedience now and when you get there is critical. This is called a *"Divine Geographical Shift"*

When you begin to experience and realize you are at the **BRINK OF GOD'S FAVOR**, remember the one and only *"Most High God"* who gave you the creative ability and power to get wealth and success!

There ain't no stopping you "NOW" when this begins! Shout Glory!

My brothers and sisters in Christ, get in agreement with God, now and quickly! I declare to you today that this is the day that you will begin to see the *"FAVOR"* of God flowing freely and profusely into your life. The *"Floods of God's Favor"*, is releasing you beyond every barriers of limitation and holds that was placed upon your life. Expect supernatural turnaround and increase of joy, healing and miracles in Jesus name!

Prophetic Prayer and Declaration #14
"Brink of Favor"

Lord I thank you that you are a covenant keeping God, thank you for your promises and divine protection and guidance. As you were with Abraham servant on his assignment to find a wife for Isaac, I decree and declare that you are with me on the God-given assignment you have established through this ministry and my life.

I decree and declare that, as I walk before you in obedience, you have sent your angels to be with me and to prosper me.

I thank you that I will not be blind-sighted by distraction or my own agenda because I have carefully submitted all my plans to you and I am led by your Spirit.

Lord I thank you that, I am at the "***Brink of God's Favor***" and it is about to overflow its banks into my life. "***Floods of Favor, Floods of Good Breaks, Floods of Supernatural Miracles, and Floods of Kindness***" coming to me "***NOW***" in Jesus name.

I decree and declare that today marks the turning point of God's overwhelming favor being outpoured into my life, my family, ministry and business projects and opportunities.

I decree and declare that I am being released beyond every barrier of limitation and holds placed upon my life, family, ministry and business projects and opportunities.

I decree and declare supernatural turnaround now of God's insurmountable blessings, increase of joy, healing and mercy in Jesus name.

I decree and declare that I have positioned myself to do God's will therefore the manifestation and flood of his overwhelming favor and promises are coming into fulfillment right now in my life in the name of Jesus!

I declare and declare this day that I am at "*The Brink of Favor*." I decree and declare that I am about to enter into the **"FLOOD OF GOD'S FAVOR"** without limitations. I decree and declare that God has in store for me "**FLOODS OF BLESSINGS**" coming into my "***DESTINY***" in the name of Jesus!

I decree and declare that I am about to

experience debt cancellation and promotions. I decree and declare I am about to meet that right person for my life and ministry. I decree and declare new open doors for business and ministry opportunities!

I decree and declare that because of my obedience I have entered into a *"**Divine Shift**"* Globally, territorially, regionally, nationally and personally of the "***FLOOD OF GOD'S FAVOR***." I decree and declare that my continued obedience will maintain this constant flow of God's *"**Floods of Favor**."*

I decree and declare that I will not forget who gave me the creative ability and power to get these good breaks, to experience these overwhelming *"**FLOODS of FAVOR**"* in my life in the name of Jesus.

I decree and declare that there is no stopping me **"NOW"** the **"FLOODS OF GOD'S FAVOR"** has overtaken every area of my life now in Jesus name! Glory, Hallelujah! I decree and declare that I am in agreement with heavens decree through this Prophetic Word today in the name of Jesus.

I decree and declare that today is the day that I will begin to see the *"FAVOR"* of God freely flowing profusely into your life, releasing you beyond every barriers of limitation and holds that was placed upon my life in the name of Jesus.

I decree and declare that I expect supernatural turnaround and increase of joy, healing and mercy in Jesus name!

I thank you for angelic protection and for making my way prosperous in Jesus name, Amen!

Prophetic Prayer and Declaration #15

Take It Back Praise

Exhortation

Psalm 107:7 says, *"He led them by a straight way to a city where they could settle."*

Let us slowdown from our busy activities of life during this time on God's Calendar to offer up praises and thanksgiving with joy for how he has delivered you in the past and even presently! He deserves all the praise and glory in our lives.

What are you waiting for begin to praise him! Praise Him right now and enter into the **"SHIFT"** because as you praise Him you will begin to drink and draw water out of the wells of salvation. As the scripture says, the joy of the Lord is your strength.

1. Take your strength back.

2. Take your joy back from the devil!

3. Take you peace back!

- It's your deliverance!
- It's your healing!
- It's your breakthrough!
- It's your blessings!

NOW TAKE IT BACK. With high praises in your mouth and with the two-edged sword in your hands [the word of God. Conquer and repossess the promises of the Lord to you and your household with a ***"MARATHON OF PRAISES."*** Shout Glory!!! ALLELUJAH!!!

Let everything that have breath PRAISE THE LORD, PRAISE YE THE LORD!

#praisebreak #dancing #singing #footstomping #handclapping #soundofthetrumpets.

Prophetic Prayer Declaration

Thank you Lord according to Isaiah 12:3 that *"with joy I shall draw water out of the wells of salvation."*

I decree and declare that this is my season of abundance, my season of the overflow of God's overwhelming favor, power and provision, without delay!

I decree and declare that with high praises in my mouth and with the two-edged sword in my hands [the word of God] that I here now conquer and repossess the promises of the Lord to me and my household and with a *"MARATHON OF PRAISES" "TAKE IT BACK"* in the name of Jesus!

I decree and declare that:-

- It's my deliverance!
- It's my healing,
- It's my breakthrough!
- It's my blessings!

I decree and declare that with my praises, I take them all back in the name of Jesus. I decree and declare that there is a "**SHIFT**" in the atmosphere with my praises and songs of deliverance and:-

- I TAKE MY STRENGTH BACK.
- I TAKE MY PEACE BACK.
- I TAKE MY JOY BACK in the name of Jesus.

I TAKE IT ALL BACK with my **PRAISES,** singing the highest praises! ALLELUJAH!!! ALLELUJAH!!! In Jesus name – Amen.

Prophetic Prayer and Declaration #16
Lord I Just Want To Say "Thank You"

John 16:33 *"I have said these things to you, that in me you may have peace. In the world you will have tribulation. But take heart; I have overcome the world."*

Hallelujah!!! Lord I love you, Singing Hallelujah because even in the tough times of test and trials I am able to draw closer and trust you more, singing Hallelujah! It's the highest praise. Thank you that you are my peace.

I decree and declare your goodness and mercy. In the world I may experience tribulation, but I thank you that I can rejoice and rest in your peace that you have already overcome the world.

Lord I thank you that the whole duty of man is to worship you alone, the one true and living God and my soul is just crying out Hallelujah!!! I am so grateful and I thank you for you "*Peace*" Mighty God. Thank you for surrounding me and my family with your overwhelming goodness and peace!

Thank you that there is no sorrow in serving you! My soul bless the Lord and worship His Holy name. I decree and declare, bless the Lord ~ Oh my soul ~ I will worship your Holy name.

I decree and declare that, every knee shall bow and every tongue must confess that Jesus Christ is Lord.

I extol you Lord, what a mighty God we serve, angels bow before Him, heaven and earth adore Him what a mighty God we serve!

I pay homage to you Lord declaring that you are the Most High God! Oh magnify the Lord with me and let us exalt His name forever! I sought the Lord and He heard me and deliver me from all my fears.

I decree and declare that no more will trials and tribulations and not being sure of what the future holds for me or being afraid of the unknown rob me of my *"Peace!"*

I stand upon your word that, I shall not *"be anxious about anything, but in everything by prayer and supplication with thanksgiving let your requests be made known to God. And the peace of God, which surpasses all understanding, will guard your hearts and your minds in Christ Jesus."*

I decree and declare that I make my request known to you today therefore I let go and let God have His way in my heart, my mind and soul! I thank you for this time of refreshing in your presence!

I thank you Lord, for renewing my mind today with the hope and assurance that you are my *"Peace"* and I worship you oh Lord!

I decree and declare the *"Aaronic Blessings"* of Numbers 6:24-26 upon my life and my children's life that, *"The Lord bless thee, and keep thee: The Lord make his face shine upon thee, and be gracious unto thee: The Lord lift up his countenance upon thee, and give thee peace,"* both now and forever more - In Jesus name! Amen!

Prophetic Prayer and Declaration #17

The Spirit of Courage

"But I am full of the courage that the LORD's Spirit gives, and have a strong commitment to justice. This enables me to confront Jacob with its rebellion, and Israel with its sin" [Micah 3:8].

I decree and declare that the Spirit of wisdom, understanding rest upon me, and the counsel of the Lord. I decree and declare that God has not given me a spirit of fear but of power, love and of a sound mind.

I decree and declare that I have the Spirit of Christ living on the inside of me through my adoption to Sonship and by Him I cry 'Abba Father'.

I decree and declare that that the Spirit of Sonship solidifies my faith and confidence that the Spirit of the Lord has given me **"Faith That Dominates"** and in every situation I am more than a conqueror, for John 1:12 declares, *"**For as many have received him to them have ye power to be me the sons of God.**"*

I give you praise for the Spirit of courage and the fear of the Lord in Jesus name, Amen.

Prophetic Prayer and Declaration #18

I Am Strong In Your Grace

Lord I thank you that David declared in Psalm 27:3 that, ***"Though an host should encamp against me, my heart shall not fear: though war should rise against me, in this will I be confident."***

Thank you for the confidence and hope I have in you that gives me assurance that you are my sustainer. Therefore, I decree and declare that because you are my sustainer you make me strong.

Thank you that because I am strong in your grace, my kingdom and personal relationships will be lasting and remain warm despite difficulties.

I decree and declare that I am made fully transformed from the strength in your grace that gives me the strongest force and power to act as a Kingdom Ambassador representing you at all levels in the kingdom.

I decree and declare that I am strong in your grace that makes me fortified so as to protect me against the attacks of my enemies in Jesus name.

I decree and declare that I am strong in your grace that makes me a leader who governs and exercise with authority and power against threats, forces or violence in Jesus name.

I decree and declare that, I am strong in your grace and I will not be easily influence by others.

I decree and declare that, I am fortified, resolute and determined like David to dwell in the house of the Lord and in the secret place of the Most High God in the name of Jesus.

I decree and declare that, I am spiritually fortified and always in a spiritual defensive position against enemy forces because I am made strong and confident in your grace.

I decree and declare that, you are the Most High God and I am strong in your grace. Therefore I am not easily deterred by danger or pain.

I decree and declare that I am strong in your grace that makes me courageous.

Therefore, I possess and have the capacity to hold and contain the Exousia power in Jesus name.

I decree and declare that I am strong in your grace, possessing the spirit of excellence and authority to keep and maintain my inheritance as *"The Kingdom of Heaven suffereth violence and violent take it by force."* In Jesus name! Amen - Shout Hallelujah!!!

Prophetic Prayer and Declaration #19

Fearless Faith

2 Timothy 1:7 says *"God gave us his Spirit. And the Spirit doesn't make us weak and fearful. Instead, the Spirit gives us power and love. He helps us control ourselves."*

Lord I thank you that, you hath not given us the spirit of fear, but of power, and of love and of a sound mind. Father I thank you that you sent your son Jesus Christ to die on the cross for our sins is a reflection of true love.

I pray that your love will radiate through me continually inspite of how others treat me. Lord I forgive those that have taken me for granted, rejected, neglected and ignore me that I thought understood and know this God of Love.

Lord many times I am tempted to seclude myself because of how others take for granted this touchstone privilege we have as believers to demonstrate your love as a profession of our "*FAITH*."

Lord I thank you for continuing to strengthen me to continually serve and demonstrate as a leader, minister of the Gospel, and woman of God your *"Agape"* Love, inspite of the challenges and test of my "*Faith*" that comes with my Kingdom Assignment.

I decree and declare that your love oh Lord is unselfish and unwaveringly sacrificial in the giving of yourself. Therefore, I shall continue to be the reflection of the *"Faith"* I have in you.

Lord I forgive those that have hurt me in anyway or form, because:-

- Love is the touchstone [Evidence] of our professed faith in Christ.
- Love is not self-seeking to neglect or ignore others, or hurt others, it holds no grudge/envy.

I pray for my brothers and sisters that are struggling to constantly and equally demonstrate this love to others that they yield themselves to the Holy Spirit and willing to lay aside their selfish agenda and innuendos and walk in forgiveness and love.

I pray that the root scars from abuse, hurts, abandonment and rejection be broken over every believer struggling to walk in this *"God Kind of Love."*

I pray that every barrier they have placed around their heart to seclude themselves because of past hurt, abuse and abandonment be broken in Jesus name!

Lord inspite of the things that comes to test my *"GOD KIND OF LOVE"* in everything that I say and do:-Let your "*Love*" emanates through me and be the touchstone of the profession of my *"Faith"* in you in Jesus name! Amen!

Prophetic Prayer and Declaration #20
Greater Is Now

Ephesians 3:20 declares *"Now unto Him who is able to do exceedingly, abundantly, far able all You can ask or think according to the power that worketh in us"*, so I thank you Lord for my miracles!

I decree and declare that "**GREATER IS NOW**." I decree and declare that my blessings will multiply exceedingly in this season and not dwindle.

I decree and declare that I am the head not the tail - above and not beneath:

I decree and declare that I shall possess a large supply of God's wisdom, knowledge, revelation, tangible blessings and spiritual increase.

I decree and declare that there shall be to a great extent an extreme supply of all I need above and beyond my greatest expectation according to the power of God that works in me and through me in Jesus name, amen.

Prophetic Prayer and Declaration #21
The Battle Is The Lord's

2 Chronicles 20:15 declares, *"He said, "Listen, all you people of Judah and Jerusalem! Listen, King Jehoshaphat! This is what the LORD says: Do not be afraid! Don't be discouraged by this mighty army, for the battle is not yours, but God's."*

I decree and declare that I shall not be afraid of this great multitude for the battle is not mine it is the Lord's.

I thank you Lord for reminding me not to take the battle into my hands!

I decree and declare that, my wrestle is not against flesh and blood but against principalities and powers, rules of darkness and spiritual wickedness in high places.

Therefore, I guard my heart with all diligence for out of it flows the issues of life. I decree and declare that my praise and worship is a gateway to my breakthrough and blessings.

I decree and declare that I am refocused, repositioned and renewed to rest in the Lord of the battle!

I decree and declare that in this season my worship unto the Lord has repositioned me to "*Seize the Moment*" and reclaim as well as repossess my wealthy places in the name of Jesus.

I decree and declare that you have given me the power to create wealth.

I decree and declare that I am blessed and my territory is being enlarged in the name of Jesus.

I decree and declare that what you have promised me and my children I am able to achieve and accomplish because my praise goes before the battle.

I will therefore stand still and see the salvation of the Lord Jesus Christ in my life in Jesus name, Amen!

Prophetic Prayer and Declaration #22
I Am Full of Power By The Spirit

Micah 3:8 declares, *"But truly I am full of power by the Spirit of the Lord, And of justice and might, To declare to Jacob his transgression And to Israel his sin."*

I decree and declare that the Spirit of wisdom, and understanding rest upon me and the counsel of the Lord!

I decree and declare the Lord has filled me with the Holy boldness of the Lord: - Filled with justice and strength to boldly declare God's word and demonstrate His power!

I decree and declare that he has not given me a spirit of fear but of power, love and of a sound mind!

I decree and declare that I have the Spirit of Christ living on the inside of me through my adoption into Sonship! And by Him I cry

"Abba Father."

I decree and declare that I have **"Divine Access"** through Sonship! I decree and declare that I have the **"Faith that Dominates"** and in every situation I am more than a conqueror - for as many has receive Him to them gave ye power to become the Sons of God, in Jesus name - Amen!

A Publication of

Apostle Dr. Nadine Manning Global Ministries Inc.

(1)   Awake To Your Destiny – Volume 1
        ~ "The Mind of Christ."
(2)   "I Am Anointed For This." – Awake
        To Your Destiny ~ Volume 2
(3)   I Am Anointed For This Prophetic
        Unlocking.
(4)   The Prophetic Unlocking –
        Intercessors Devotional – Series 101

Sermons and Prophetic Prayer Teaching and Declaration available on CDs and DVDs

You can write, call our email me at:-
Apostle Dr. Nadine Manning
P.O. Box 91, Millville, New Jersey 08332.
Email: - *apostlenadineglobal@gmail.com* or
nadinehmanning@gmail.com.

Website: - ***Apostlenadineglobal.com***
Telephone: - 609-972-6346 or 856-825-8280.

Apostle, Dr. Nadine Manning for: -

Preaching/Teaching, Conferences, Workshops,
Revivals or Spiritual Warfare and Deliverance Prayer
Services or Revivals, please email us at
Apostlenadineglobal@gmail.com

www.ingramcontent.com/pod-product-compliance
Lightning Source LLC
Chambersburg PA
CBHW060116050426
42448CB00010B/1886